bloom wild

a free-spirited guide
to decorating with floral patterns

BARI J. ACKERMAN

PHOTOGRAPHY BY CARLEY PAGE SUMMERS

ABRAMS, NEW YORK

FOR MY MOTHER, Betty Palles, who informed my style
with her eclectic décor, demonstrated creativity
in everything she did, and inspired my love for flowers.
And for my grown children, Anna and Emily, so they can
see that absolutely anything is possible. I love you!

CONTENTS

SECTION THREE

the garden house

introduction

YOU LOVE FLORALS and you want to decorate with them, but maybe you're not sure how. I'm here to tell you that you can rock the florals in a minimal or a maximalist way depending on your desires, and it's not hard—so forget your worries about what goes with what, looking too granny, or looking too wild, and get ready to dive in.

In this book I will show you all I've learned from decorating and living with florals my whole life. You can go head-over-heels crazy for them, or just pop a sweet floral in a surprising place to add panache. It's really up to you.

My love affair with florals started in childhood. My mom loved all floral patterns. We'd see them everywhere at home: She had Desert Rose everyday china and Rose Chintz china for special occasions. She had a botanical carpet going up the stairs and a floral tole chandelier in the kitchen, and my own room was wallpapered in a tiny rose print. I spent months when I was about six years old watching my mom create a giant needlepoint bouquet that still hangs above my parents' bed. And my mom, like I do now, painted florals. Floral décor is part of who I am.

Flowers themselves bring on a certain nostalgia for me as well. Maybe they do for you, too. Do you have memories of gardening as a child? Did a grandparent have a special garden that you reminisce about? The front of our house had rows of tulips each spring and the side was lined with peony trees. In one house, there was a row of lilac bushes I miss desperately here in Arizona. I used to bring my teachers lilacs cut from those bushes wrapped in a wet paper towel and tinfoil. I can still remember their sweet scent.

Growing up in this environment made floral décor a part of my psyche. It's not even something I think about. It's just what I love.

Maybe you are just jumping into decorating with florals or you've always wanted to but didn't know how. I hope that my passion for flowers sparks the same in you. I encourage you to be bold and brave in your decorating choices. Do what speaks to you . . . you'll learn to refine and edit as you go along. It makes me so happy to be part of your floral journey!

BLOOMING INSPIRATION

A home should truly reflect who you are. It holds your memories and all the things you love. It's a place you should enjoy to the fullest. Whether you love florals but just need a little help making them work together or want to incorporate even more florals in your design, the starting point is to find some beautiful and diverse inspiration and then start layering the pieces you love to create a look all your own.

CHAPTER 1

find your floral vibe

how to discover your own style

bloom wild

Begin by exploring the immediate world around you. Study your current surroundings and really take them in. I'll be the first to admit I haven't done nearly enough traveling. But you can give any day a sense of adventure travel if you view your surroundings in a new light.

LILACS

Lilacs, with their almost melodious scent, are said to be associated with youthful femininity. They also mark the beginning of summer—and of love, according to experts on the meanings of flowers. Lilacs have a special meaning to me because they offer a sense of both nostalgia and renewal.

GARDENS AND PARKS

When travel isn't an option, there are lots of places to look for floral inspiration right at home. The place you live likely has a local botanical garden or even a plant-filled park or conservatory. I grew up in suburban Chicago, Illinois, and love the botanical garden there. It is such a rich resource. Here in Phoenix, the Desert Botanical Garden is filled with inspiration. We recently visited the botanical garden in San Francisco. I could walk around these Zen spots for hours on end. When you go, always take lots of photos—this is useful for creating an idea board. Plus, you can easily have your photos enlarged and printed to create large-scale wall art or even a series of photos for a gallery wall. A photo of a place you've enjoyed will make you happy every time you pass it. (More on that in chapter 12!)

The same goes for walks around your neighborhood. Take a really good look around you. Take in the quiet and observe. Walk more slowly than usual. You are sure to be surprised at what you see when you stop and literally smell the roses. Even a snapshot can turn out beautifully and become art for your home. You'll also start to recognize flowers that you see regularly, and images of those will become more meaningful pieces to put in your home.

MUSEUMS

Next stop: museums. My very favorite way to visit a museum is by myself. With no one else to answer to, I can roam and daydream without distractions. Take a look and discover who your favorite artists are. Look at historic textiles, ceramics, sculptures, photographs. You'll start to really hone in on what you love. I once spent an entire day by myself in the textile room at the Victoria and Albert Museum in London while my husband was in the city on business. It was a day I'll always remember. I kept notes on what I saw and took photos where allowed. I also stopped in the museum shop and picked up a book with more information on the exhibits. To me, this is a heavenly and inspiring way to spend a day. I always visit the gift shop as well. I'll often find museum postcards with images of things I couldn't take photos of, which I like to take home for inspiration.

As a substitute, I've also been known to search museum archives online. For instance, the Smithsonian Institute's website (si.edu) is searchable. I simply typed the word "floral" in the search box and thousands of images popped up. By searching "Monet" on the Art Institute of Chicago's website (artic.edu), I easily found all the Monet art in the museum's collections. Check your favorite museum's website to see if they have a search feature. We are so blessed to live in a time when everything is at our fingertips. Of course, a trip to see the art in person is even better, but when you can't do that, why not take a peek at these wonderful resources?

LIBRARIES AND BOOKSTORES

If you don't have a museum nearby, get thee to the good old-fashioned library! There you can browse through volumes of art and gardening books and find ideas in countless pages. Of course, bookstores are another obvious place to go for inspiration. I have a ridiculous number of art and home décor books. I love simply having these on my coffee table. Paging through them when I'm lacking a creative spark always turns the lightbulb on and gets me going.

FLOWER SHOPS

Another spot that fills me with happiness and creativity is a flower shop. Be sure to talk to the florist and ask about the flowers. I've found that even in a grocery store, the people who work at the flower stands are knowledgeable and can offer loads of information about the flowers. Of course, also ask if it's okay to take photos. And again, take notes.

Now, you may be wondering why I didn't suggest using a general search engine like Google or a social media site like Pinterest to search for images of flowers. That is a good idea, and we will use it for a project at the end of this chapter, but these sites have algorithms that allow only the most popular content to float to the top. Often that makes what you find relatively homogenous. You'll see the same images over and over again. I find this disables my creativity. And the speed at which I surf around the web doesn't allow me to take much in. That's why my favorite suggestions involve really getting out in the world and taking in as much as you can while disconnected from technology.

pattern notebook: using a mood board

CREATING A MOOD BOARD keeps me on track: I can refer to it in the midst of a decorating project, and it helps keep the design goal clear. So, before you dive headfirst into a project, I recommend creating a mood board. Whether your board is online or on a poster board, a bulletin board, or even directly on a wall, the materials and colors will encourage you (and a fun collage on a board or a wall can even serve as décor itself).

DIGITAL MOOD BOARD

Often when starting a project, I go to Pinterest. I type in search words relevant to what I've already learned I love out in the real world (as opposed to what the Pinterest algorithm decides to show me), and I start pinning. Pin anything and everything you love. When you've got a full board, curate it. See which images on your board are similar. What have you pinned over and over? Keep that and delete everything else. The benefit of a digital board is that you can refer to it on a smartphone or tablet when you're out and about shopping.

COLLAGE MOOD BOARD

Gather up all your favorite magazine clippings and photos printed from your travels and field trips. Armed with information that you gathered in the real world, you can also search the internet and print items you like for your own use. Cut out the images, flowers, and colors you love. Once you have plenty gathered, start curating. What is the through line in what you picked out? Is there a certain color you see over and over? A certain flower? A type of image? Those are the things to put on your mood board, and likely will be things you highlight in your design.

fundamental floral formulas

mixing and matching floral patterns

bloom wild

I learned how to mix florals with other patterns by designing floral prints and fabrics. I'm always thinking about how I want to use the designs that I create. A lot of my prints are used for interiors so I'm very conscious of that. I'll think, "How will this work on a pillow, and what would I put with it," "What would this look like as drapes," or "How would this work as a pattern for wallpaper or upholstery?"

PEONY

The peony is said to be a symbol of good fortune and happy marriages. They are a traditional twelfth-wedding anniversary present. With their large petals, peonies also represent compassion. In China, peonies symbolize nobility.

OF COURSE YOU DON'T have to create collections for fabric, wallpaper, and home products to become skilled at mixing and layering patterns. Usually, when I am working on a collection, there are ten prints in two colors (we call them "colorways") each. I think of the prints as a "hero" (the main event), a "ditzy" (small flowers), or a "stripe"—and a great floral design mixes all three together.

When designing a collection or a room, I begin with a "hero" or "focal" print. This is the main print in a collection—and, for interiors, the one you want to stand out the most. For me, that print is usually a large, allover floral. (Allover means the direction of the motif goes in all directions.)

DITZY

After the allover "hero" print, I'll add a smaller, "ditzy" floral. ("Ditzy" means the print has tiny repeating flowers or bouquets, usually scattered throughout the print as opposed to in a row or a stripe.) Ditzy patterns often look like a solid color fabric at a distance, making them a great versatile print. Because their motifs are small, ditzy florals are an easy print to use to dip your toe into floral décor. If you love a minimal look but want some florals as well, this is a great place to start. When you pair a large-scale floral with a ditzy, you have a beautiful contrast.

STRIPES AND GEOMETRICS

Next, I add geometrics and stripes. This can be an obvious stripe or a floral mimicking a stripe. Some patterns—such as the prints on the following page—have vertical lines that mirror a stripe repeat and can be used just like a traditional stripe.

Geometrics are any pattern with dots, triangles, squares, or other shapes in a repeat. Stripes and geometrics both contrast florals.

FLOWERS THAT WORK
AS STRIPES AND DOTS

All three of the florals at left are laid out in a vertical fashion, so when you use them against an allover pattern, they create contrast.

The same goes for dots. Instead of a classic dot pattern, try using a pattern with a single floral repeat, like the fabrics shown here. The little flowers work as dots and create contrast with other patterns.

ANIMAL PRINT NEUTRALS

When possible, it is fun to add an animal print. Leopard print works as a neutral and varies the scale in a group of prints. Look how cool it looks with this chinoiserie-style print. There's a touch of the leopard print colors in the main print. The leopard print would work great as an accent like the welting on a pillow or a little skirt on an upholstered chair.

STYLE MIX

I also vary art style and technique when creating a collection, and you can do the same in your pattern mix to give your design energy. For instance, the gray floral pattern here is based on a painting. The yellow floral on top was created as a graphic illustration. They are both florals, but their style contrast is intriguing. As you can see, one feels more organic than the other. This creates visual interest in your décor.

CLASSIC LUXURY

I will often incorporate something that reads as a damask. A true damask is a luxurious reversible fabric, usually silk or linen, with a pattern woven into it. "Damask" literally means "to decorate or weave with rich patterns." Damasks typically have motifs such as leafy wreaths and garlands in a vertical repeat.

CHINOISERIE

Chinoiserie prints are another style I adore. *Chinoiserie* is a French word that is derived from *chinois*, which is French for "Chinese." Chinoiserie prints tend to be European interpretations of Chinese themes. They are usually scenic and focused on nature in subject. I like to use these in home décor because the designs tend to be more asymmetrical and have more flowing open space. This helps to build contrast in a fabric collection and, of course, in décor.

BLENDER PRINTS

Another pattern I like to incorporate in a collection is a "blender." Sometimes this can be a print that is tone on tone, meaning the design is a variation of the background tone, with flowers as a motif (like the turquoise print at left). Other times it can be something that is a textural pattern like this "scratch" print (the light blue fabric on the bottom). A blender offers flexibility in a collection of fabrics and gives the eye a place to rest. It's the negative space between the florals that lets the florals shine.

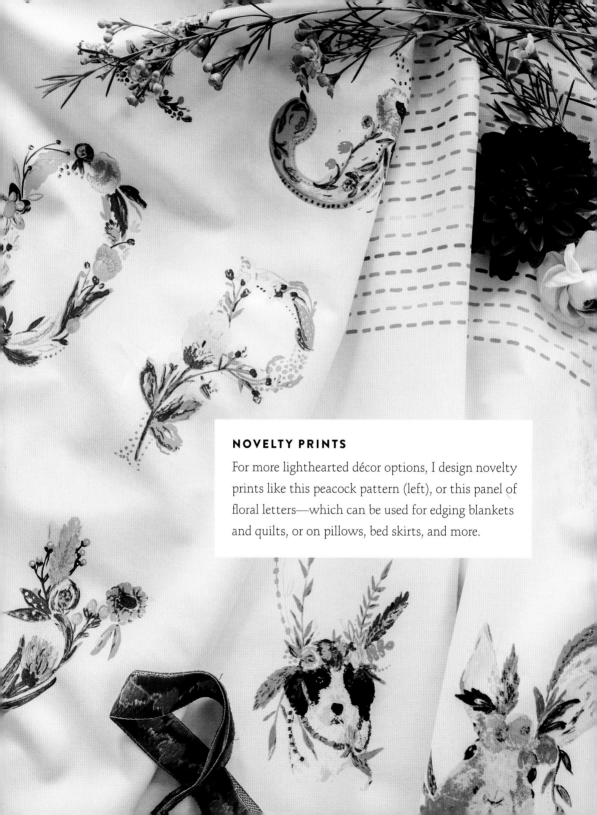

NOVELTY PRINTS

For more lighthearted décor options, I design novelty prints like this peacock pattern (left), or this panel of floral letters—which can be used for edging blankets and quilts, or on pillows, bed skirts, and more.

mixing & matching patterns

NOW THAT YOU KNOW what all these prints are, let's condense things into an easy formula you can use when shopping for fabrics, wallpaper, bedding, and more.

Here's my mantra: Florals go with stripes and leopard print goes with everything. I'm not playing when I say this. I mean it. People often say, "You're so bold when it comes to mixing fabrics. I'm too scared to do that." I promise you, it's much easier than you think. When mixing and matching on your own, think about *contrasts* and *through lines*.

Two patterns together should contrast, but there should also be something that ties them together—I call this a "through line."

When you mix a large floral with a tiny floral, there is contrast between the two. If there is a similar shape or color tying the two together (the through line), that makes it a great match. A large floral can also mix with a geometric print (contrast) if they have a color or two in common (a through line) to tie them together. Likewise, a pattern that looks painted goes great with one that has a more digital look to it—as long as you tie the two together with a color or a shape.

It's always about a contrast and a through line.

Now let's take a look at a few things that work while being unexpected.

the magic equation:

contrast + through line =

pattern–mixing success!

UNEXPECTED COMBINATIONS

If ever two prints "shouldn't" go together—but do—
it's this leopard print and floral. But look closely. The
scales contrast, but they have both colors and shapes
in common.

contrast

+

common
color

+

shape

=

harmony

STRIPE + SCALLOP × COMMON HUE

We should also look at the stripe and the scallop in the middle pillow here. Stripes are always a great contrast, but as you can see, the colors from the floral are in there. And the scale of the scallop is noticeably different than the leopard print and the stripe, but it carries through the pink hue. All of which make seemingly disparate patterns work together.

COLORS FROM A PAINTING +
ACCESSORIES = PERFECT ACCENTS

Now let's take a peek at a design for a master
bedroom. It seems I break my own rules here. Why
does pink work? It's surprising, but it does. With the
painting, the more obvious choice would be to add
blue bedding and accessories, right? I initially tried
that, but it ended up looking pretty dull. So, I tried
the less obvious route. Capitalizing on the greens and
the yellows in the painting, I added green pillows
and a mustard-colored pillow. The hot pink, while
surprising, has a black background—so it adds some
pop while still tying into the colors in the room.
There are four patterns in this design, each one a
different scale and each picking up a color from the
painting. That's what makes the room—and the
pattern mix—a success.

What's most important, though, is to try to set aside
your adult self and just play as if you were a child. Is it
pleasing to your eye? Keep it. If you are questioning it,
you're probably not there yet. Keep playing.

fundamental floral formulas

pattern maps

I OFTEN SEE people work with fabric that was created as a collection, but you don't have to do that. Use fabric scraps to map out a mix of patterns, and to experiment with scale and color.

MATERIALS

Fabric scraps
Notebook or paper surface
Adhesive

TO MAKE:

1   Pattern maps help you mix and match on a small scale, before you commit to a big fabric purchase. To create a pattern map, make the first step a game: collect a bunch of scraps or samples of fabric that you like.

2   Line up the fabric swatches, then mix and match them.

3   Put together combinations that please you, then adhere them to a page in your notebook or glue them to a piece of paper.

4   You can also take a field trip to a fabric store and play. Walk around the store and really look at the colors, shapes, and patterns—then pull out fabrics and patterns from different parts of the store and put them together.

5   Pretend you are planning to have some pillows made. What would you use as the main fabric, and what might you choose for a contrast welting or ruffle? Try a large-scale floral and then see if there's a stripe with a color in the floral that could be used as the contrast.

pattern notebook

THINK ABOUT TWO OR THREE fabrics you might use as a group of pillows. Find a large-, medium-, and small-scale floral that have something in common. Find a geometric that might also contrast. All you have to do is keep contrast and through line in mind. Look for both contrasts and one thing that ties the elements together. Eventually your eye will get used to doing this and it will become second nature. Most of all, don't be afraid to make mistakes. I used to walk into a fabric store and feel incredibly intimidated. I thought there were rules! I can assure you, there are no real rules. If you like it, it's probably just right!

Now that you've done this in a fabric store, you'll also be able to do this when you are shopping for finished goods such as bedding, drapes, and wallpaper. You'll no longer have to pick from one collection that was made to go together. You'll be able to mix and match—and create a small-scale Pattern Map before you commit to a large purchase. Just because something was made as a set doesn't mean you have to purchase it as a set. If you want your décor to be a real reflection of who you are, shopping multiple collections in multiple places should be your new go-to.

OPPOSITE Coordinating large-, medium-, and small-scale florals. THIS PAGE Here large-, medium-, and small-scale florals coordinate with the striped pattern.

a little floral science and ritual

the facts behind our passion for flowers

I often wonder why flowers attract us. It's universal. They are pretty, of course, but surely there is more to it. To me, flowers are the physical embodiment of joy. I have long believed that there must be a scientific reason that a beautiful bouquet always makes people smile. And it turns out there's actually science to back up that theory!

RANUNCULUS

Across many cultures and generations, the ranunculus flower symbolizes charm and attractiveness. Traditionally, giving ranunculus to someone tells them you think they are radiant and charming.

bloom wild

ACCORDING TO RESEARCHERS, much of the enjoyment flowers inspire comes from chemicals in the brain tied to our evolution: Gatherers knew that the appearance of brightly colored flowers meant the season of abundance was coming and food would soon be plentiful. Our brains actually release dopamine (a brain chemical that creates feelings of happiness) when we see flowers.

Other studies found that hospital patients with flowers and plants in their rooms actually reported lower pain and had lower blood pressure, among other positive results. Naturally, then, we gravitate toward offering flowers to our loved ones to make them feel better.

Knowing that florals and floral scents truly do lift the spirit and support healing, we instinctively bring beautiful bouquets into our homes, give them to our loved ones, offer them as gifts when we go to someone's home, and use the scents as perfume. Flowers are woven into our lives because they truly inspire positive emotions.

a little floral science and ritual

ESSENTIAL OILS

Recently, we've seen a rise in the use of essential oils from flowers. I've used them in my home for years, but was only vaguely aware of their proper uses. Wanting to know more, I asked my friend Desha Peacock, a passionate essential oils expert and businesswoman who conducts amazing creative retreats.

Desha highlighted something we know instinctively: floral scents have an effect on your mood, and they have been used for centuries to heal the mind, body, and spirit. She also encourages users to choose natural oils over synthetic ones, in order to reap the maximum health benefits from the plant or flower.

Some of Desha's and my own favorite essential oils are:

ROSE: Opens the heart to receive divine love.

JASMINE: An aphrodisiac, encourages intimacy and self-acceptance.

YLANG-YLANG: The oil of the inner child; encourages playfulness and sharpens intuition. (I think this one is especially good for creativity!)

Desha recommends mixing any of these florals with your favorite citrus (lemon, wild orange, tangerine, bergamot, or lime) to calm anxiety, purify the air, and lift your mood. Oils can be applied directly to the skin or used in a diffuser to fill your rooms with their scent.

FLORAL AND BOTANICAL SMUDGES

Also popular is the use of floral and botanical smudges, a ritual that comes from ancient Native American tradition. Smudges are bundled bits of dried botanicals: Sage, cedar, lavender, osha root, sweetgrass, and mugwort are said to be particularly powerful. To use a smudge, light the end with a candle and then blow out the flame, allowing the herbs to smolder. Holding the smoldering bundle, walk around the space with a clear intention and mind, using a feather to waft the scent in the air. Use this ritual to clear negative energy from a space (particularly before you move in or if there has been a negative event or person in the space). Personally, I use smudges to help focus on an important task, or when I feel there has been some bad energy in my life. That may sound a little "woo-woo," but to me the ritual and the scent are a way of marking the start or end of something. It's simply a mind-set. The scent alone changes my mood, and performing the physical act of spreading the scent helps me feel I've moved forward or ended whatever it was I needed to end. (To put out a smudge, crush the burning end into a plate or bowl with a bit of sand in it. Be sure not to use a plastic container.) Plus, the smudge bundles are super pretty to have around.

FLORAL HISTORY AND THE MEANING OF FLOWERS

We may not always recognize it, but flowers play an important role in our lives. We pick wildflowers and grow cutting gardens. We use flowers in both weddings and funerals. Flowers are given to celebrate births and birthdays. They are a universal expression of love. The Victorians assigned symbolic meaning to flowers—and created whole books and dictionaries on the "language" of flowers and floral bouquets. These books were designed for admiration and display, and also intended to be studied: Every young lady hoped to be fluent enough to understand the meaning of flowers received from an admirer. Today, of course, we don't necessarily attach specific meanings to individual flowers. However, understanding floral symbolism is wonderful food for thought when decorating with floral patterns. Throughout this book, you'll find sidebars with the meanings ascribed to various flowers to offer you lovely reminders of the past and to add meaning to your décor.

how to make a floral smudge

BEFORE YOU BEGIN, here are a few plants that work well in a smudge and are commonly burned. (If you are using other plant materials, make sure—before you burn anything—that the resulting smoke is safe and nontoxic. Always arrange for good ventilation before lighting a smudge.)

SAGE Used for clearing negative energy.

CEDAR Used for protection.

PINE NEEDLES Used for cleansing and purification.

SWEETGRASS Use after a cleansing smudge to attract positive energy.

MUGWORT Used for calming and purification.

ROSEMARY Used for protection.

ROSE PETALS Used for meditation and calming. Also attracts love.

PEPPERMINT Used for healing.

MATERIALS

Bouquet of fresh sage, lavender, and rosemary
A few roses and other flowers of your choosing (optional, for decorative bundles)
Baker's twine
Burlap (optional)
Matches or a lighter
Feather (optional)
Small dish filled with sand

(continued on page 61)

TO MAKE:

1 Gather the plants you would like to bundle and trim the ends of the stems to the same length.

2 Arrange in a pleasing bouquet.

3 Wrap the bundle in baker's twine as shown or wrap the stems with burlap first and then tie with twine.

4 Allow the bundle to dry in the sun for a week.

5 Place the bundle in a significant spot as a decorative talisman—or move to the next step and use it as a smudge.

TO SMUDGE:

1 Use a match or lighter to ignite the bundle.

2 After letting it burn for a few seconds, blow out the bundle. It will continue to smolder.

3 As the bundle smolders, walk around the space you wish to smudge and fan the smoke with a single feather (optional), focusing on your intention. Native Americans and other cultures view feathers as having come from a higher realm. If you do find a feather on the ground to use, be sure to "wash" it with sage smoke. Sage smoke will cause mites on the feather to die and help to preserve the feather for future use.

4 Completely extinguish the bundle in the dish of sand. Many people use an abalone shell with sand for this as the shell and sand represent the sea while the herbs represent the earth. (Never leave a bundle smoldering.)

USING TEXTILES TO MAKE YOUR SPACE BLOOM WILD

Here is how to begin layering, mixing, and matching blooming textiles in every room of the house. Textiles are my starting point in décor not only because I design them, but because they can be used in such a wide variety of ways. This section will show you how and where to use them. And you'll see real-life examples of the mixing–and–matching principles I describe in the first part of this book.

CHAPTER 4

three essential floral prints

the floral trio I can't live without

I believe that when you are picking floral prints there are three that are essential. These should be your go-tos when you are shopping. The first is a large allover floral with a packed design (meaning not much space between the motifs); next, a medium to large floral with a loose design (space between the motifs); and last, a small or ditzy floral (see page 25).

DAHLIA

Having started out as an exotic bloom seen in aristocratic gardens, the dahlia later became fashionable in gardens all over Britain. Flower enthusiasts say the dahlia commonly symbolizes grace under pressure and inner strength. Dahlias come in a wide variety of bright colors and white.

ANY OF THESE LARGE ALLOVER FLORALS would make a strong focal point.

A large floral can be the focal point for an entire room. But it may leave you wondering what to pair with it. Let's experiment with some florals and put them together for a cohesive yet fun look.

On the two pages that follow you will see three examples of large-, medium-, and small-scale florals working well together.

FEEL THE DIFFERENCE | artgalleryfabrics.com

MY THREE ESSENTIAL FLORALS

I love these three because you can use them all together in many different color schemes and they will always contrast one another beautifully—which is the key to mixing prints successfully. (For more on contrast and through line, see chapter 2.)

WHY ARE THESE A MATCH? The largest-scale print in each fabric has colors that are also in the other two prints. There are even some similar shapes. But because every print is a different scale, each one stands on its own and does not blend into the others. Proof that you can't go wrong if you stick with the three essentials. You may throw in a chinoiserie or a geometric pattern, but you can mix with confidence as long as you choose three differing scales and link them with similar colors and/or shapes.

THE FABRICS shown all mix and match gracefully, thanks to the common color palette and varied scale of their floral patterns.

IN THIS QUILT-AND-PILLOW COMBO, you see the formula in action: The pillow features a large allover floral with a ditzy floral piping, and there are a few medium prints in the quilt. Geometrics are thrown into the mix as well to open the space and add further contrast.

Ditzy florals can work a myriad of ways. On a quilt, the ditzy could be the piece that reads as somewhat solid. On curtains, it can be used as trim or maybe as a section at the top or bottom.

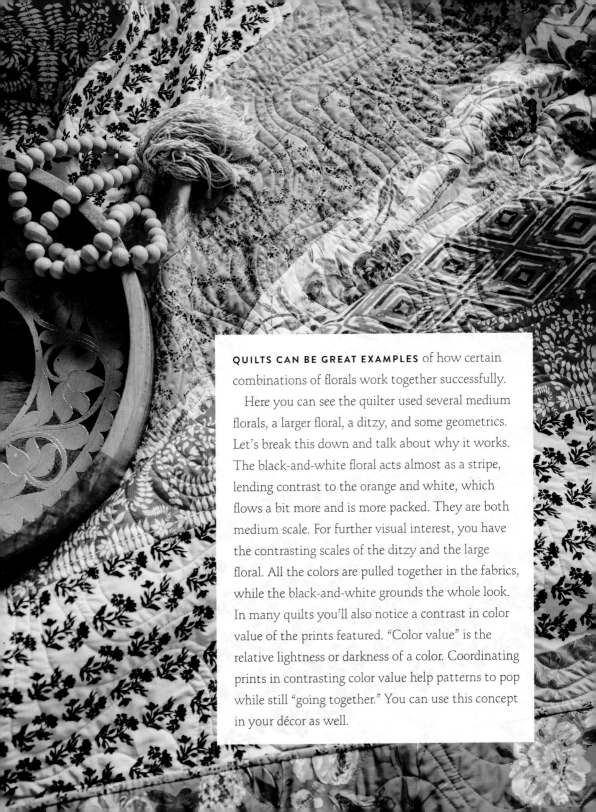

QUILTS CAN BE GREAT EXAMPLES of how certain combinations of florals work together successfully.

Here you can see the quilter used several medium florals, a larger floral, a ditzy, and some geometrics. Let's break this down and talk about why it works. The black-and-white floral acts almost as a stripe, lending contrast to the orange and white, which flows a bit more and is more packed. They are both medium scale. For further visual interest, you have the contrasting scales of the ditzy and the large floral. All the colors are pulled together in the fabrics, while the black-and-white grounds the whole look. In many quilts you'll also notice a contrast in color value of the prints featured. "Color value" is the relative lightness or darkness of a color. Coordinating prints in contrasting color value help patterns to pop while still "going together." You can use this concept in your décor as well.

TONAL PRINTS—such as the blue geometric and yellow floral here—are blender patterns that will read as a solid color. They work beautifully with large-, medium-, or small-scale floral prints.

secrets of styling with pillows

pattern–filled displays for every space

bloom wild

The truth of the matter is, I probably need a pillow intervention over at my house—I now have a closet in the guestroom entirely devoted to pillows. However, it can't be overstated: Pillows are the easiest way to update décor. They're so versatile. They come in all shapes, sizes, colors, and prints, offering almost endless possibilities for combination.

ROSE

The rose has been known as a symbol of love since the earliest of times, say flower enthusiasts. Venus, the Roman goddess of love, is thought to have been accompanied by roses at birth. The roses shown are a special breed of David Austin roses.

YOU CAN PURCHASE solid-color pillows almost anywhere, or, if you'd rather go handmade, making your own pillows can be an absolute breeze. Best of all, most pillow shapes only require you to sew simple, straight seams. I'll explain exactly how to make a pillow at the end of this chapter.

Pillows are my go-to when it comes to creating a custom look. I think one of the best design tricks is the "high/low mix," which means pairing expensive items with affordable ones and chain store purchases with unique vintage and handmade items. The result is a collected, curated look that you can't get by simply shopping in retail stores. Adding pillows to the mix is super fun and easy.

There's so much to choose from: round pillows with tufting, square pillows, bolsters of all sizes, even custom shapes such as triangles. You can add trim such as fringe and tassels, piping, binding, and more. And if you don't want to sew, that's not a problem. Custom décor is surprisingly obtainable. A quick internet search will pinpoint a local upholsterer who can stitch your pillow designs for you. Mix those special pieces with store-bought items, and voilà! You have a look that's all your own.

To make it all easier for you, it's a good idea to study several designs for inspiration. Remember, keep your design cohesive by using both contrasting and similar (through line) elements whenever you mix and match.

one sofa, four ways

AHHH! THE SOFA. My favorite spot for changing it up! Styling your sofa can be confusing. Should you pile all the pillows on? Or use just a few? How should you space pillows on the sofa? Which prints go together? Here are four different ways I styled my own family room sofa—I hope they will spark lots of ideas for your own space.

MATERIALS

You will need:
A sofa or loveseat
A throw (optional)

FOR CASUAL BALANCE
3 round pillows, 2 square pillows

FOR THE MOTIF MIX
3 square pillows (one a solid color)

FOR THE COORDINATED COLLECTION
1 large square pillow, 1 medium square pillow, 1 small rectangular pillow, plus 2 coordinating pillows of your choice

FOR MODERN GEOMETRY
5, 7, or any odd number of pillows in a mix of sizes and shapes

cultivating your own pillow recipes

CASUAL BALANCE

The first look features a pair of round pillows in matching vintage 1950s fabric mixed with a single solid-color velvet pillow. You'll notice that an odd number (whether of pillows or other accessories) creates a more interesting look than grouping together an even number of pieces. The other trick I use here is also simple: Accent a collection of patterned pillows with one solid pillow (or vice versa). Designers use both of these techniques to create a balanced yet casual look. (Additionally, a suzani throw on the back of the sofa reflects the colors in the pillows here while also adding contrast—since the suzani is a different style and scale.)

COORDINATED COLLECTION

This look mixes three pillows of different sizes and shapes. While the pillows differ in size and shape, their fabrics are from a single fabric collection ("Virtuosa") and they each have the same piping, to pull the look together. While the fabric colors harmonize, the scales of the prints vary. The geometric print gives the collection a modern, fresh feel. With three pillows at one end of the sofa, I added just two coordinating pillows to the other corner—again, for an odd number of items.

MOTIF MIX

For the third grouping, I repeated three pillows in one corner, but this time I brought back the green velvet pillow and mixed it with two green florals of differing styles. The pillow farthest to the right is a vintage bark cloth in a chinoiserie style. The green floral to the left is a more open large floral. The mix works because the motifs have different but complementary scales.

MODERN GEOMETRY

This look incorporates some really fun geometric pieces into the mix, as well as a solid. Solid colors break up the pattern and give your gaze a place to rest. Again, note the differing scales of the geometrics and solids.

USE PILLOWS TO CREATE A BOHO LOOK

When I think of boho, I immediately picture a
caravan filled with collected and handmade items.
Worn vintage fabrics and fun details complete
the look. My recipe for boho pillows includes the
following ingredients: fringe, tassels, pom-poms,
embroidery, hand stitching, a bit of patchwork, and
a mix of old and new fabrics.

This fun outdoor dining scene was craving some
happy, boho flair, so I piled up loads of pillows in
every style—notice the crochet fringe on the pillow
fronts and seams, and the pillows adorned with
vintage lace (I used loads of vintage fabric for this
collection). To transform pillows you already own,
add tassels on all four corners or all the way around,
and embellish with stitching (such as on the green,
lavender, and orange kantha pillow on the following
page) for a handcrafted look.

THIS OUTDOOR SCENE can be replicated indoors as well. Surround a large coffee table with floor pillows of every shape, and then scatter in a few throws. Make sure tassels, fringe, and pom-poms abound. In my view, this combination makes a great setup for a teen lounge or college apartment.

Details such as hand stitching, tassels, fringe, and lace suggest old-world bohemian style.

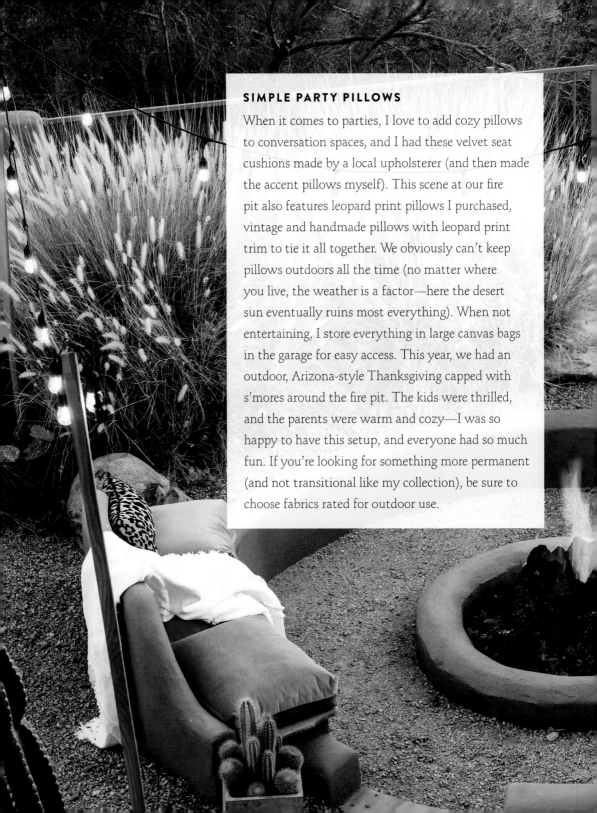

SIMPLE PARTY PILLOWS

When it comes to parties, I love to add cozy pillows to conversation spaces, and I had these velvet seat cushions made by a local upholsterer (and then made the accent pillows myself). This scene at our fire pit also features leopard print pillows I purchased, vintage and handmade pillows with leopard print trim to tie it all together. We obviously can't keep pillows outdoors all the time (no matter where you live, the weather is a factor—here the desert sun eventually ruins most everything). When not entertaining, I store everything in large canvas bags in the garage for easy access. This year, we had an outdoor, Arizona-style Thanksgiving capped with s'mores around the fire pit. The kids were thrilled, and the parents were warm and cozy—I was so happy to have this setup, and everyone had so much fun. If you're looking for something more permanent (and not transitional like my collection), be sure to choose fabrics rated for outdoor use.

PILLOWS FOR A NAPPING SPACE

If you love the idea of creating little spots of respite in your home, you can't beat a pillow-stacked daybed. Here, for example, I carved out a little napping/reading spot in the corner of our guestroom. I kept the look very simple and cozy with a large tasseled floral pillow, a pillow created from a vintage needlepoint, plus one twin-size pillow for a sleepy afternoon. Things to note: One pillow is an allover floral, the other is a single motif. Both are on black backgrounds. This is what makes the pillows work together.

how to make an envelope–back pillow

MATERIALS

1 yard (1 m) of fabric
1 yard (1 m) fusible fleece
22-inch (55 cm) pillow form/insert
Thread
Sewing machine

TO MAKE:

1   Cut out one 22-inch (55 cm) square of fabric and one 22-inch (55 cm) square of fusible fleece (this will be the pillow front).

2   Cut out two 17 x 22-inch (42.5 x 55 cm) pieces of fabric and one 17 x 22-inch (42.5 x 55 cm) piece of fusible fleece (these will create the envelope back).

3   Fuse the fleece to the wrong side of each piece of fabric according to the manufacturer's instructions.

4   For the two pieces that form the envelope back, you'll want to hem the edges that will be exposed. Along one 22-inch edge of each overlapping piece, fold toward the wrong side of the fabric by ¼-inch twice (shown at left). The raw edge will then not be seen. With the folded edge up, top stitch along the entire edge to hem.

5   Place the fabric for the pillow front right-side up on your work surface.

6   Now you'll put it all together. Place the pillow front on your table right side up. Put the two envelope pieces on top (overlapping one another), right sides facing the pillow front. The edges you just hemmed will be on the inside and the raw edges of the envelope pieces will be aligned to the raw edges of the pillow front. Pin all the way around the pillow.

7   Using a ½-inch (1.5 cm) seam allowance, sew together the pillow front and envelope back.

8   Trim the corners to (but not through) the seam line and turn the pillow case right-side out. Press.

9   Insert your pillow form through the envelope back.

cultivating your own pillow recipes

tabletop blooms
settings bursting with blossoms

If you are like me, a pretty tablescape makes your heart sing. The mixture of tabletop textiles, dishware, glasses, and artistically displayed food is both eye-catching and delightful, whether for entertaining or for every day. Naturally, I think this is the perfect place to go full-on maximalist because it can be for just a day. If you want to give floral patterns a try but can't quite commit, here's your chance to invite your inner maximalist to glow.

GLADIOLUS

The gladiolus is regarded as a symbol of strength of character and integrity. It has been written that gladioli were the flowers of the gladiators, and they have been associated with swords. They make a beautiful, colorful backdrop in the garden.

1. Be sure to mix
and match.

2. Layer textiles
for a dynamic table.

3. Vary the height of
centerpieces and accessories
to add interest.

4. Use trays, plates, and
bowls to anchor
centerpiece accessories.

5. More is more!
(Truth! I say this about
almost everything.)

tabletop blooms

EVERYDAY TABLE RECIPES

In the kitchen, I like to keep it relatively simple so that we can actually use the table each night for dinner. When the table isn't set for a meal, I'll often have a tablecloth, a runner, and a little something in the middle. I love cloth napkins for environmental reasons but also because they're just so pretty. I'll keep cloth napkins set on my casual dining table for visual interest.

It's just plain fun to change the look. Throw a fabric tablecloth on for variety, or layer tablecloths, runners, and place mats. Don't be afraid to mix and match. Just go back to the guidelines: Vary scale and pattern while using a color or a shape to tie things together from piece to piece.

For centerpieces that are semi-permanent (not for a holiday or a party), I'll sometimes fill vintage tins with small flower arrangements (I line them with plastic cups cut to fit, plastic storage containers, or even disposable plastic zip bags so they won't leak or rust). Other times I'll just put a series of candlesticks in the middle of the table. And sometimes I place a wooden tray or a cake stand in the center and top it with a few glass bottles full of flowers plus essentials such as the sugar bowl and salt and pepper shakers.

When decorating the table, don't forget about other elements in the room. For instance, there's a floral rug in my kitchen, so the textiles I use on the table have to vary in scale to the pattern on the rug, but pick up its color palette. (I also like to change the chair pads every once in a while, from solids to a ditzy floral print.)

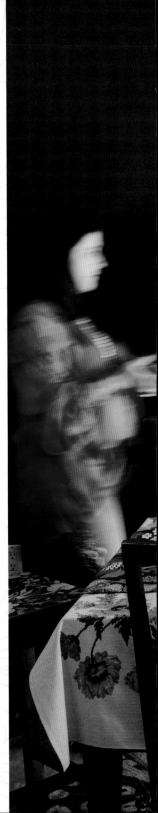

**THINGS TO KEEP ON HAND
FOR CREATING TABLESCAPES**

Apothecary jars

Vintage tins

Vintage glass bottles

Wooden bowls and trays

Glass cloches

Cake stands

Cheesecloth (You can dye
cheesecloth and casually rumple
it across a table for a fun and
super-affordable element.)

Placemats, chargers, runners,
napkins, and tablecloths

Fabric (I've been known to layer
raw-edged unhemmed fabric
on a table in a pinch. Force the
edges to fray a little more for
a nice worn look.)

SETTING THE TABLE

Here are the designs for four unique tablescapes to try on your own. The "casual blooming table" (page 104) can be used daily or for a simple dinner with friends. The "flourishing brunch table" (page 105) makes a great setting for bridal and baby showers or even a lovely Sunday brunch just because. The "maximalist floral dining table" (page 106) goes all the way with mixing and matching floral patterns, and "fresh patterns for dining alfresco" (page 113) is full of ideas for outdoor dining that are lively and fun.

THE CASUAL BLOOMING TABLE

For this casual dining table, I used a vintage
tablecloth with a golden floral border topped with
vintage fabric as a runner. (Instead of cutting into
the many vintage fabrics I keep on hand, I fold them
to use as a runner or leave them open to use as a
tablecloth.) For a little whimsy, I simply tied squares
of fabric in knots and set them on top of the plates
to be used as napkins. I kept these a simple striped
pattern for easy mixing and matching. If the pads on
your kitchen chairs will be in use most of the time,
as mine are, you may want to cover them in a ditzy
floral for added interest. Here I chose a tiny print in
colors I regularly use in my tablescapes.

THE FLOURISHING BRUNCH TABLE

What's better than brunch? Setting the table for brunch! I love to have the ladies get together every once in a while, and I've amassed a collection of vintage china for those occasions. Not much is more pleasing to me than mixing and matching vintage china patterns. Here I topped the table with a piece of vintage floral fabric and added an array of serving dishes. One thing I truly love is juxtaposing modern flatware with old-fashioned china and fabrics. Try it—it makes for a very charming table. In fact, don't ever be afraid to mix modern and vintage anything— as a rule, do!

A MAXIMALIST FLORAL DINING TABLE

The very first thing that went on our wedding registry twenty-five years ago was a classic William Morris–patterned china. (Though I didn't know it at the time, even back then my style was maximalist and I liked over-the-top blooms!) In the department store where I put together my registry, they had a table set up with an enormous bouquet of flowers and my china sitting on woven chargers. My mother was with me, and I turned to her and said, "THAT!" Her response was, "I don't know if you'll like that in twenty-five years." Naturally rebellious, I dug right in and put the pattern on my registry. Today, these dishes (shown opposite and on the following two spreads) still light my fire when I see them. When I saw the pattern, I knew it was a classic and would never go out of style, and I also knew I was going to treasure it forever. That instinct, I now realize, was rooted in a lifelong passion for maximalist prints. Listen to those instincts. Buy what you love even if it doesn't make practical sense—when you know, you know.

IN A FORMAL DINING ROOM, you can go to town mixing and matching to your heart's content. For this setting, I made place mats from a rich, lushly patterned paper, then layered on napkins in a complementary color. The floral napkins have a pattern that is slightly larger and airier than the pattern on the place mats. Notice how the William Morris dishes feature the smallest print on the table, and the basket chargers plus vintage glassware add interesting textures to the arrangement. I used modern flatware to give this setup a fresh look.

VINTAGE-INSPIRED

The raspberry tablecloth pictured here has a border print, which runs along the edges, perfect for a tablecloth. I layered it with a floral table runner for a more maximalist vibe. Tassels at the end of the runner add extra visual interest. The casual dinnerware (inherited from my mother) features a pattern called Desert Rose, and it inspired the hand-painted napkins and charming hand-painted glasses.

FRESH PATTERNS FOR DINING ALFRESCO

Most places have seasonal opportunities for outdoor dining—and in the Arizona desert, that is almost all year. One of my fabric collections, "Sage," is actually based on the blooms of the desert.

how to make your table bloom

IT'S TIME TO get your inner maximalista on. Since a tablescape doesn't have to be permanent, here's where "more is more" can shine.

bloom wild

MATERIALS

A large print floral tablecloth or solid fabric
Floral runner
Plates and dishes in a contrasting floral
   or a solid
Napkins in a ditzy or other floral print
Bouquet of flowers

TO MAKE:

1 First, cover the table with the tablecloth or solid fabric to create a base.

2 Next, add the floral runner, then set the table with the dishes you have chosen.

3 Layer in the napkins. Napkins are fun to play with, so try setting them between dishes, placing them on top of dishes, or even tying them in a simple knot.

4 Last, add fresh flowers as a finishing touch. Keep in mind my mixing-and-matching guidelines. Once again, this is all about having fun. There is no wrong way to set a maximalist table.

CHAPTER 7

blooming furnishings
flowers add the finishing touch

You can make your furniture part of your indoor garden with slipcovers and upholstery. If you don't know how to sew, no problem. You can usually find a local upholsterer to stitch professional slipcovers or reupholster furniture for you. I do this a lot when I just don't want to sew.

HYDRANGEA

Hydrangeas can symbolize so many things—some negative and some positive—that they must be paired with another flower so the recipient will understand the intention behind the gift. We wouldn't want an expression of heartfelt emotion to be confused with heartlessness (just two of the symbolic interpretations for hydrangea).

FLOWERY OTTOMANS, STOOLS, AND BENCHES

Footstools and benches are among my favorite things to cover in floral fabric: Doing so is not a huge commitment—and since they are accents, they won't steal the limelight, even in a room with lots of other florals. You can find all kinds of great little pieces to re-cover at discount home furnishing stores and thrift shops. Oftentimes you can find a plain bench or footstool that is very easy to reinvent: Just remove the seat or the top and staple on some new fabric (as I did here). These little pieces look great in every room. I leave one in each bedroom, there's one next to the tub and a few in our family room.

MANY FOOTSTOOLS REQUIRE very minimal effort to slipcover, since there is just a single seam around the top and one on the side. As you can see, the finished cover slips easily over the top of the stool, like a small hat. For trim, you can go with a no-sew solution: Use fabric glue, such as Fabri-Tac, to add embellishments.

CHAIRS

If you are anything like me, you've never met a chair you didn't like. I bring them home from thrift stores or even salvage them from the side of the road occasionally. I sometimes upholster or slipcover them myself, other times I hire a professional. (And I've gotten creative and sold a few when I wanted a new design.) If you are tempted to try some sassy floral upholstery, start with slipper chairs—they add lots of style and are easy to change for different looks. The pair shown at left are from a chain store and have two sets of slipcovers—a chinoiserie-style print with pretty geometric welting and (this page) a cover with a mix of floral and patchwork.

ONE OF THE (MANY) great things about slipcovers is that you can always take them off to wash them—and, naturally, you have lots of options to swap in and out.

This chair was a bit of a larger project, but it is a good example of how easy and cost effective it is to have a thrifted chair reupholstered. You'll be surprised, I promise. The fabric is canvas with a very simple line-drawn floral pattern.

WHEN RE-COVERING this Louis chair, I used a striking geometric print and added a large-scale floral pillow in a tiny size. You don't always have to make the floral the focus—in this case, I made the floral a small accent and went bold with the geometric pattern. I bought this particular chair for a very low price at a garage sale many years ago. I've since had it re-covered twice. Re-covering is also easier on the environment than buying a brand-new chair. When possible, I like to save a chair from joining tossed junk in a landfill.

OUTDOOR FURNITURE IS super fun to change up; a fresh pattern will completely transform the piece. If you're using canvas (as I did on this chair) rather than a fabric created specifically for outdoor use, be sure to coat the fabric with a weatherproofing spray (with UV protectant to protect from rain and sun) and/or cover the furnishings when they are not in use.

THE SETTEE PICTURED here was initially covered in a boring beige fabric, so I re-covered it in a lemon print and then covered the matching chairs in a magnolia pattern. To tie the two together, I put magnolia pillows on the lemon settee. And of course, never one to leave well enough alone, I added floral pillows to take it all up a notch.

make your own upholstered bench

I THOUGHT 11 x 36 inches (28 x 90 cm) was a perfect narrow bench size, but choose a size that fits your space and needs. Your local big box home improvement store can cut wood to size for you. Be sure to get a softer wood so it's easy to screw the legs in; particle board is good. For the foam, I cut down a mattress topper, which was much less expensive than the foam you find in craft stores.

MATERIALS

1 wooden board, cut to your preferred size (I used an 11 x 36-inch / 28 x 90 cm piece)

Fabri-Tac glue

1- to 2-inch-thick (2.5 to 5 cm) foam, cut to the size of your board (see Notes)

1 piece of fabric and 2 pieces of batting each cut 6 inches larger than the board both in length and width

Industrial staple gun (preferably a power staple gun, as opposed to a hand stapler)

4 (16-inch / 40 cm) hairpin bench legs

Washer hardware

TO MAKE:

1   Glue the foam to the top of your board with Fabri-Tac and allow to dry for about a half hour or according to the glue manufacturer's instructions.

2   Place the fabric wrong-side up on your work surface and place the two pieces of batting on top.

3   Place the board foam-side down on top of the batting.

4   Starting at the center of one long edge, wrap the fabric and batting up and over the board edges and onto the back side of the board. Staple in place at the center of each long side and then at the center of each short side.

(continued on page 133)

5   For the corners, at first look it seems like you should fold like you would a present around the edges. Resist that urge. Instead, as you get to the corners, stretch and taper the fabric, stapling as you go.

6   Staple all of the fabric onto the back of the board with a staple in each spot about 2 inches apart and 1 to 2 inches away from the edge of the board.

7   Trim off as much excess fabric and batting as you can.

8   Screw the hairpin legs into each corner. You'll be screwing partially into fabric on the edges, which means the leg may not lay flat. The part that is over the fabric will sit higher while another bit sits over just wood. If left like this your leg will be tilted. If this is the case for you, slip a washer or two (depending on how uneven the leg is sitting) under the screw hole that is bare of fabric and batting. You'll place the screw through the hole and the washer to level out the height.

CHAPTER 8

asleep in the garden
restful spaces for relaxing

bloom wild

When it comes to bedrooms, I think they should be as restful as a garden sanctuary. For me, flowers and blooms are natural healers. They're an absolute must in the bedroom, the place where we heal our minds and bodies from the stresses of the day. In addition to floral prints, try using a scented-oil diffuser to heighten the sense of calm respite.

FREESIA

This delicate bloom is one of the world's most popular flowers due to its sweet fragrance. Since the 1950s, freesias have been used as a wedding flower because they represent trust. Multi-colored freesia bouquets make wonderful gifts because the flower also signifies friendship and thoughtfulness.

A BOTANICAL MASTER BEDROOM

Pattern, color, and pillows are key elements in this relaxing sanctuary. Floral pillows tend to get rotated around the house quite a bit, so I always keep at least one white quilt on hand as a base. White makes it easy to change the other fabrics and colors in the room. For this particular look, I decided to play up the wall art by using matching fabric for the three pillows in the back. For a little breath of air between patterns, I added solid-color linen king-size shams adorned with coordinating floral prints and then a long bolster in a geometric pattern to finish the look. The white quilt beneath the top quilt adds another margin of breathing space, while the floral on the turndown ties back to the floral in the linen pillows. For a little luxe, there's a velvet duvet. One thing to note here is the addition of pinks and purples—adding a pop of color that doesn't "match" produces visual interest that you would not have otherwise.

A CHARMING CHILD'S ROOM

Where else can you go floral crazy if not in a child's room? My sister and I created a super-fun and colorful look and a bit of a dollhouse effect in my niece's room. The pink bedding takes a cue from the wallpaper while the print on the duvet is a medium-scale floral with lots of white space to give the eye the tiniest rest. The sweet banner spells out her name.

THERE ARE LOADS of great ways to add a floral punch to a child's room. Look for vintage items for styling, think about covering lampshades and what you might use to adorn windows. Pillows add comfort and happy highlights to a space. In this room, I couldn't resist adding lots of playful accents: a fun vintage floral mirror, an old pot-metal lamp with a fabric-covered shade, vintage floral children's suitcases, a piece of art featuring a single motif, and a few fun pillows (including one that has the same swan as the art in the frame, but in different colors). I've also added a joyous wall hanging on the door.

YOU'LL DEFINITELY WANT to think about floral accents that might personalize the space. In this room I gave Millie Rose a sweet banner with her name in floral letters. My niece loves girlie things, so a pretty dress form done up in a vintage 1950s dress and petticoat adds a little icing to the cake. When three-year-old Millie saw the finished room, she was very worried that the dress form wasn't going to stay there. We think that's her favorite part. The lesson is to dream up special flowery goodies you can add to make a child's room playful and fun. That's the absolute best part of decorating for kids!

THE GARDEN NAPPING SPACE

Creating a napping space outdoors naturally involves a hammock. I usually grab a few flowery pillows and quilts for an extra-cozy afternoon. I toyed with tying the hammock to a big tree out back but then decided it should be mobile, so we hung it on a stand. Lots of times it's by the pool; other times you can find it on the patio or under the tree. We bring out a small ottoman to hold drinks, snacks, and books, and now everyone in the family argues over who gets the hammock.

one bed, five ways

GUESTROOMS ARE ideal spots to try a change of floral scenery from time to time. If you're not sure where to start, begin with a neutral base, keeping the walls and trim white so you can change art and bedding easily. Here I've created five distinct looks in the same room, but the possibilities are endless!

QUILTED COMFORT

This design takes its cues from the quilt and layers a large-scale piece of art behind the headboard for interest. Notice the combination of different scales in the fabric prints. I used a long bolster on the bed, making it an uncrowded, cozy space in which to relax.

RUFFLED SPLENDOR

Ruffled bedding is a great shortcut for a lush look. The cane bed and loads of ruffles adorning the duvet cover dictated a simpler approach to the accent pillows. Notice the large array of prints and, again, lots of variation in color and scale. The geometric pillows at the head of the bed add an unexpected visual pop.

COOL AND MOODY BLUES

The quilt featured here is the same one you saw in the quilted comfort look (previous page), just reversed. Whenever you can, choose versatile pieces like this one. The flip side— paired with a few solid pillows to break up the patterned pillows—creates an entirely different aesthetic.

BOHO LUXE

I don't like to play favorites, but I'm particularly fond of this design. I have owned this vintage crazy quilt for ages—it's one of my most prized possessions. The fabrics are mostly dress fabrics sewn together by hand and adorned with embroidery stitches. It's such a great example of mixing and matching florals, geometrics, and solids, and shows that you really can go a little over the top and still have a great design. With so much pattern and joy going on in the quilt, I've paired it with mostly geometric and solid pillows. This look fills me with joy! I encourage you to experiment and have fun with all your bedding choices.

DAINTY FLORALS AND BOLD GEOMETRICS

Don't be afraid to try a stark contrast: Here the small-scale floral-print bedspread plays beautifully with the large geometric pillow and the two solid citron back pillows. The green throw on the bed ties into the hues in the bulletin board by the side of the bed.

pattern notebook:
easy bedroom makeover

GATHER UP ALL THE PILLOWS, blankets, scarves, and duvets in your home that might work in your bedroom. (Shopping your own home for what you have allows you to get creative without spending anything.) Think outside the box. Is there a rug that could be repurposed to accessorize the foot of your bed? Can you lay a twin duvet lengthwise across a king bed for a pop of color? Do you have throws you could add? Maybe there's an old curtain laying around that you could remake and use as a bed accent. Try fabric-based items you wouldn't traditionally use as bedding. Sometimes you just don't know until you see them in action. Mix and match to your heart's content. This kind of play will allow you to see what you like best. I always take photos as I go along so I can remember what was most pleasing to me.

THE GARDEN HOUSE

Now that you've learned to mix and match textiles like a pro, what about the rest of your home? How can you bring floral patterns to your floors and walls— or know just where to add details for a touch of charm or to make a really big statement? I'll answer these questions and more—such as, "What goes best with a bold floral rug?" and "How do you display floral art without overwhelming a space?"—in this section.

CHAPTER 9

flowering floors
beautiful blossoms underfoot

bloom wild

Flowers on flowers are great in most circumstances, but how do you make it all harmonize? Likewise, a blooming rug is a gorgeous feature in a room, but when your floor is flowering, how do you know what art and textiles to put with it? My guiding rule is contrast, contrast, contrast.

IRIS

In ancient Greece, Iris was the goddess of the rainbow. The iris flower itself inspired the fleur-de-lis of the French coat of arms, revived by Louis VII when he made the purple iris his symbol. It is one of the oldest cultivated flowers.

HERE'S HOW TO MAKE floral flooring work for your space (and while I focus much of my attention on rugs here, these guidelines will work for floral tiles, stenciled floors, and more).

In my living room, I have floral pillows on my sofa and a floral painting on the wall (a closer look of this painting is on page 206). Why do these pieces work together? It all goes back to contrast and through line, naturally. On the pillows, the spacing of the floral is wider than that in the pattern on the floor. The scale and spacing of motifs contrast. Meanwhile, the colors coordinate. The pillows have a green background, and there's green in the rug. I've added contrast with a solid pillow here as well.

That said, what ties the two together? The colors. What about the art? Why does that work? First, of course, the scale is totally different. Second, the art picks up colors—pink and green—from both the sofa and the rug. I used the pink and green as the base for the room, and then wove the colors throughout.

What other styles of art could work in this space? An abstract piece with the same colors could do the trick; a large vintage botanical print might also work well—really anything floral with a contrasting scale and spacing to the patterned rug would do it.

In the kitchen, I have another floral rug. This time, I matched it with a group of vintage floral still lifes. The scale of the florals is varied and the theme contrasts with the pattern on the floor, but the colors tie it all together. I also chose a single large vase as an accent, a strong addition. If you like mixing florals and geometrics, a plain geometric print reflecting some of the hues in the rug would look great. Additionally, you might choose a figurative artwork and leave the flowers out of the paintings altogether. Notice how the fabrics on the table and seat cushions are all in shades of green, but the seat cushions have a smaller-scale pattern. It's all about choosing the right contrasts to make the mix work.

By now you know that "Contrast, contrast, contrast" is what I shout from the rooftops, so the room on the following pages that breaks the rule somewhat, may come as a surprise. The rug features an allover pattern and the wallpaper is also a tight design. To be honest, when I first thought of mixing this wallpaper (with its compact design) and this rug (with its strong, allover pattern), I thought, "Yeah, I don't know about this . . . ," but I went ahead and did it anyway—and I'm glad I did. These wild and crazy patterns work together: The dark wallpaper and the pink wallpaper offer contrast in scale, while the floral rug picks up the color palette in yet another scale. Plus, this room is designed for children. Why not have a little fun? The takeaway: Don't be afraid to experiment with mixing and matching, as I did here. It's really all about practice and trying things out. My first instinct was iffy; I wasn't sure this would work. When I saw the combination in action, though, I became a believer!

STENCILED TILE

For the tile floor in our guest bathroom, I took a rebellious approach to stenciling—try it and it will set you free! The stencil I used is a free-form design. I simply ignored all the grout lines and painted right over them with the black-and-white stencil. If you want a more geometric look, you can use a stencil the same size as your tile, but I wanted a more free-flowing organic look. I chose plain black and white as a base so I could add colorful accents to the room. On the floor I used Rust-Oleum Chalked paint in linen white for the base and charcoal for the design, then I sealed it with four coats of Minwax Polycrylic water-based sealer (with a satin finish, to avoid a glossy look).

PROJECT
stenciled floor mats

A NICE PLACE to add a tiny pop of floral is a doormat. Here I keep the designs super simple by using a single color and a stenciled flower. I did one with an allover design (see next spread) and another with a centered motif and bits of flowers in the corners (opposite).

MATERIALS

Coir doormat

A floral stencil

Blue painter's tape (optional)

A stencil brush

Outdoor patio paint in the colors of your choice

Plastic/paper plates or containers to hold your paint

Paper towels

Spray sealer in a matte finish for outdoor use

TO MAKE:

1   Place the stencil on top of the doormat. (You can tape it down to keep it from moving as you work, but the tape may not hold on to the natural fibers well, so you'll also need to hold the stencil in place with your hand as you go.)

2   Dip your brush in paint, then dab off any excess on paper towels (this avoids flooding the stencil with paint and keeps the outline sharp).

3   Use the brush to tap the paint over the cutout portions of the stencil until you've filled in the design.

4   Allow the paint to dry according to the manufacturer's instructions.

5   Spray the doormat with the sealer and let dry according to the manufacturer's instructions before placing it in the location of your choice.

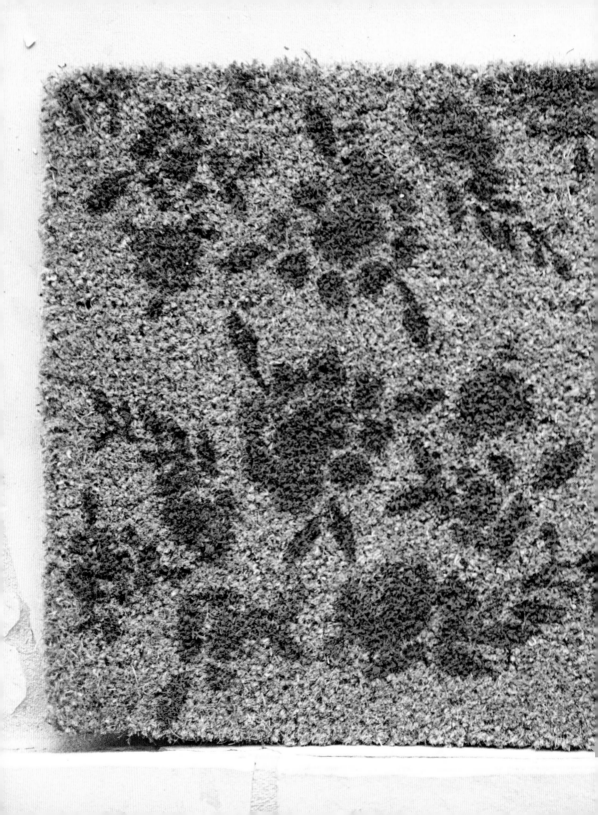

CHAPTER 10

florals that pop
pretty details for extra charm

bloom wild

If you're just getting started using florals, ease in by adding just a few as fun details. The truth is, I'll paint a floral on anything that isn't moving. I promise you can do it, too—it doesn't have to be difficult. At the end of this chapter, you'll find a simple tutorial with easy steps for painting flowers. But painting isn't the only option. There are hundreds of creative ways to let florals bloom all over your home.

TULIPS

There was a mania for tulip bulbs in seventeenth-century Holland, and prices became extraordinary. The craze made the tulip (especially blooms in bright fiery colors) symbolic of passion.

UNEXPECTED FLORAL ACCENTS

I love to reinvent everyday objects by adding surprising or unusual details. Wallpaper—especially leftover wallpaper—is pretty awesome for this purpose. The piece shown here is an old dresser I collaged with wallpaper scraps from various projects to give it a whole new life.

IN THE KITCHEN, why not line the insides of cabinets and drawers with floral paper? When I did this to our buffet, I purposely mismatched the drawer and cabinet linings (see following spread). In hidden little areas such as these, why not allow yourself a little joy? Although the liners are hidden most of the time, I'm always delighted when I open those cabinets and drawers.

OTHER PERFECT SPOTS for a dash of floral: the sides of a drawer, the inside of a pantry, and even the risers on the stairs. Many companies (including one I design wallpaper for) actually make stair riser decals, so you don't even have to trim to fit.

MORE FLORAL INSPIRATION—fabric-covered books and boxes make great accents that you can easily change with the season or on a whim.

LAST, DON'T FORGET about lampshades. Here in the kitchen, I have very little in the way of florals—the focus is on lots of moody colors with the emerald tile, black cabinets, and midcentury pendant lamps. I thought about adding another pendant above the sink, but I like to mix rather than match, so a drum-shade with a tiny splash of floral did the trick. Little details are perfect when you just need an accent and don't want to go all out.

PAINTED DETAILS

If you are like me, there is an IKEA dresser somewhere in your house. Ours is in the bedroom,
and it was plain flat white when we brought it
home—boring! I gave it a coat of gray chalk paint
and then painted on simple flowers. I kept it pretty
neutral, just tones of citron green on the gray, so I
could have flexibility in the rest of the room's décor.
Additionally, I kept the pattern serene by leaving
plenty of negative space between the flowers. If you
prefer not to hand-paint flowers, stenciling produces
a similar effect.

FLORALS ARE MIRACLE WORKERS for tired-looking wooden furniture. I had these stools for many years, and they were a pretty ugly fake cherry wood color. To give them new life, I painted them green, layered florals on top (you could stencil instead here, too), then sealed them with varnish to prevent wear.

ONCE YOU LOOK, you'll find there are countless
things you might paint with flowers. I've painted
flowers on bowls, planters, mirrors, tins, books,
napkins . . . you name it! Nothing is safe from my
paintbrush—and once you've read this book, nothing
in your home will be safe from yours!

PROJECT

painting a simple flower

YOU CERTAINLY DON'T have to be a professional artist to paint a simple flower motif. These flowers are divided into distinct parts with space between the petals. I promise you can do this! Painting can be very easy if you just break each flower down into simple shapes. As for paint, I mix it directly on the surface as I go. I'll dip one side of the brush in one color and the opposite side in another, then apply them. For this flower, our perspective is that the center of the flower is at the top and its petals billow out from there. I taught myself to paint, and so can you.

MATERIALS

Acrylic paint (I used Hansa yellow
    medium, green gold, sap green, and
    titanium white)
A filbert (oval-headed) paintbrush
A surface to paint on

TO MAKE:

1   Paint a bumpy floral center using the flat of the brush. I tend to wiggle the brush a little up and down to achieve the bumps.

2   Next use the rounded edge of your brush to paint a row of petals. You'll face the rounded part of the brush down or up depending on the petal direction. The brush shape helps you create rounded petal shapes.

3   Add a second row of petals below the first row for a larger flower.

4   You can also add a couple smaller petals above the center with the rounded parts facing upward.

5   For leaves, use the edge of the brush to paint a thin stem, then press down on the brush and pull to create the curve of a leaf.

6   Add your own flair, if you'd like!

CHAPTER 11

walls that bloom

wallpaper, murals, stencils, and hand-painted florals

Bold wallpaper or murals are traditional ways to make a statement in almost any room. But hand-painting (see page 176), stenciling (see page 160), and especially chalk florals (see page 194) are also terrific and innovative ways to give a space panache.

DAISY

The daisy is associated with the purity and simplicity of children. William Morris, one of the most revered design heroes of the Arts and Crafts movement, is said to have disliked more flamboyant flowers, much preferring the simple daisy.

MURALS

This mural is based on one of my paintings: I found a mural company online that would print a high-resolution scan of my painting to the size I wanted. Cool, right? If the resolution of the image is high enough, you can print nearly any size mural. So easy! Some ready-made murals are even printed on peel-and-stick material, so you can take them down as easily as you put them up, particularly good if you rent your home. Both custom and ready-made murals are easy ways to add huge florals to your walls for dramatic impact.

WALLPAPER

Now, here is the same studio, this time with floral wallpaper in a large-scale repeat standing in for the mural. I love both looks, but they are distinctly different from each other. Since I use this room to store supplies and fabrics in the open, I opted for a single wallpapered wall to keep the space from being too visually cluttered. (And peel-and-stick wallpaper is pretty darn awesome, especially if you are design fickle like me.)

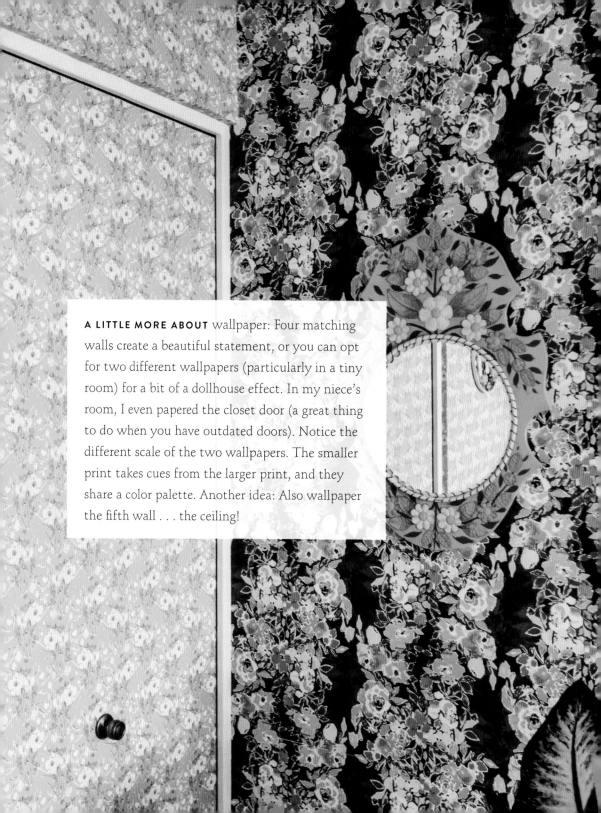

A LITTLE MORE ABOUT wallpaper: Four matching walls create a beautiful statement, or you can opt for two different wallpapers (particularly in a tiny room) for a bit of a dollhouse effect. In my niece's room, I even papered the closet door (a great thing to do when you have outdated doors). Notice the different scale of the two wallpapers. The smaller print takes cues from the larger print, and they share a color palette. Another idea: Also wallpaper the fifth wall . . . the ceiling!

NEVER ONE TO SKIP a utilitarian room, I had the whole laundry room wallpapered in a lemon botanical print.

CHALK ART

At last, the chalkboard wall! When my daughter left for college, I erased her teenage graffiti (with her permission) and drew a wall of colorful florals (see page 194 for instructions). Although they look sophisticated, DIY chalk flowers are surprisingly easy to draw. And they are not just for bedrooms—try them as an easy update for the walls of kitchens and pantries, too. You might even chalk paint a dull closet door and make it a feature of the room.

HAND-PAINTED FLORALS

For this design, I painted grayscale florals, then used
a contrasting color on the lower part of the wall. To
add even more contrast, I layered in a painting by an
artist friend, Mel Remmers. Substitute wallpaper for
the painting, if you like—there are so many beautiful
floral designs on the market—but keep in mind that
painted flowers are super easy, and you'll be surprised
at how quickly you can master the technique. To
paint something similar on your walls, use the same
technique as described on page 176.

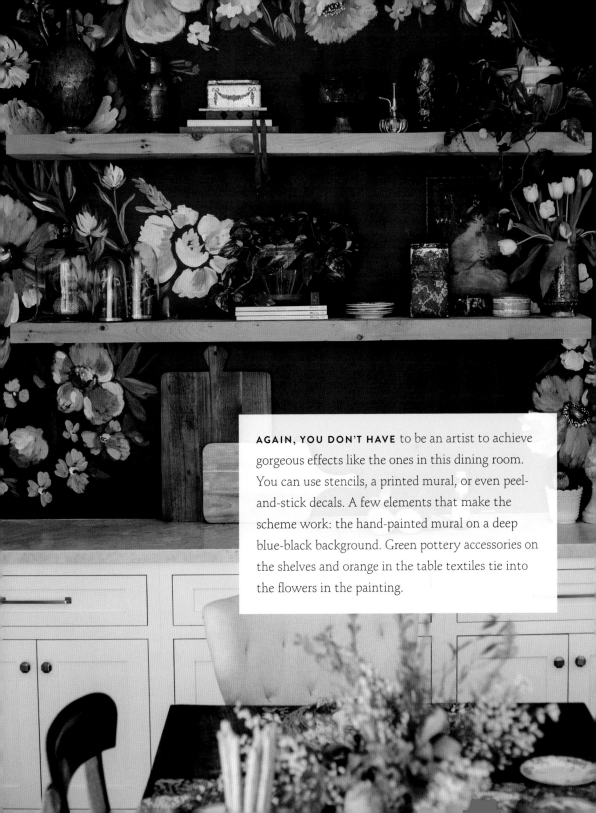

AGAIN, YOU DON'T HAVE to be an artist to achieve gorgeous effects like the ones in this dining room. You can use stencils, a printed mural, or even peel-and-stick decals. A few elements that make the scheme work: the hand-painted mural on a deep blue-black background. Green pottery accessories on the shelves and orange in the table textiles tie into the flowers in the painting.

IN THE MASTER bedroom, I also hand-painted florals on the wall using quite a similar technique. In addition, I used the art on the wall to play with layering a pattern on pattern. The floral walls extend from the painting (see the following spread). Again, the same effects can always be achieved by using stencils or wallpaper in place of handpainting. In fact, this particular design is also available in a wallpaper.

STENCILS

In a bedroom, stenciled flowers highlight a single wall. This is a very inexpensive way to add a little joy and interest to a room. And the stencil does double duty as wall art. I chose a black-and-white look for this room to make a statement without drawing too much interest away from the rest of the design.

drawing chalk flowers

AS WITH THE PAINTED FLORALS on page 176, these flowers start with a floral "center" at the top and flow out from there.

MATERIALS

A wall or other surface painted in chalk board paint

Chalk in various colors

TO MAKE:

1 Draw a simple irregular oval shape with an open bottom.

2 Add a few petals coming up around the sides.

3 Add a few more petals in a rounded shape but with irregular edges toward the bottom of the flower's center.

4 Add a row of petals flowing outward from the center.

5 Add a few more petals at the top.

6 Add a few leaves. Some of the leaves I added visibly have stems, while others peek out from behind the flowers.

7 Add shading to the flower: Simply scribble in a thicker line on the outer petals at the edges and then smudge inward. For the inner petals, create shading flowing from the other direction.

CHAPTER 12

artful flourishes
art completes the room

Now it's time to consider the art hanging on the walls. Again, it can be challenging to decide what works best in a layered floral scheme. You want the art in the room to sit harmoniously with other pieces that you've used. It's best to start by thinking about which piece in the room is the statement piece.

IF IT'S THE ART, pick that first and then pick other items to work with it. If your rug is a large allover floral, add wall art that has blooms in a smaller scale. You might want to hang art that isn't floral at all (*gasp!*). An abstract or geometric piece of art in a very layered room can be a resting place for your eye. I also love using figurative art. And, of course, you can always layer floral on floral. Here's a few techniques for getting the mix just right.

ORCHID

Orchids were a symbol of virility in ancient Greece. The Aztecs are said to have mixed the vanilla orchid with chocolate to create a potion that would reportedly promote power and strength. In Victorian times, orchids were collected to show luxury and refined taste.

FLORAL WITH FLORAL

In our kitchen, we have a large-scale floral rug. I also wanted floral art. But this can be a little tricky. Even a medium-scale floral could distract from the rug. Instead, I hung a series of vintage still lifes. The flowers depicted in the paintings differ from the rug in style and scale, but they reflect its colors, which ties everything together. The pieces are all eye-catching but don't necessarily compete for attention. You'll also notice that the colors and styles of the paintings are similar, which makes them a cohesive group. Not one to leave well enough alone, I have changed this room frequently over the years. Several times, I have replaced the gallery collection with a single large painting (see the following spread) which works well with the rug, too.

I USED THIS TINY NOOK to create a fun vignette. Since it's right near the front door, this spot is always in view. I layered a large-scale floral on a background of tiny tone-on-tone flowers that almost read as a solid. This is a nice way to successfully combine florals without distracting from the main attraction: the wall art. (As a side note, the "wallpaper" here is actually fabric. I adhered it to the wall using liquid starch. One coat of starch is applied before putting the fabric up, and a second after the fabric is on. After it dried, I trimmed the excess fabric and framed it in wood trim.)

GALLERY WALLS

Sometimes, a gallery wall adds visual clutter instead of beauty and interest. The problem can usually be solved by framing all the art in the display with the same type of frame (or a similar one). You can also make the art the common thread, displaying images that all share themes or colors or forms. The gallery display with the paintings of bouquets in vases (see pages 198–99) is one good example of the latter. Yet another approach is color blocking, as I have done with the simple trio of floral prints shown. The frames and prints are all the same, but the print colors vary.

FOR A VERY SIMPLE LOOK that is easy to re-create in many color schemes, try hanging vintage botanical prints symmetrically in a vertical series. You can choose a variety of prints, as long as you stick to botanicals—ideally from the same source or book—and keep the frames identical.

FOR WALL ART that goes full tilt maximalist, here I chose to create a gallery from art on paper by layering it on the wall using painter's tape on the back. I covered the entire wall. This can be a really fun look for an art or sewing studio, a teen lounge, or a free-spirited den. It's also a great look for a playroom wall covered in your kid's art pieces.

LARGE-SCALE ART

Displaying a very large piece of art is one of the easiest ways to create strong visual impact. There's not much measuring or planning involved, as there is with gallery walls, and less effort, too—one strong picture hanger, and you are done! Many people choose gallery wall displays because large-scale art can be costly. However, if you add up the cost of all the gallery wall pieces, you may find that a large piece is just as cost-efficient.

PHOTOGRAPHS

Photographs are a nice way to bring in visual contrast, especially if the other floral elements are painted. When you're out and about, be sure to take photos. You never know when one will come in handy for your décor. There are all sorts of places that will print photos for very reasonable prices. I had this flower market photo printed on glass, to bring in textural as well as visual contrast.

LITTLE POPS OF ART

Never underestimate small pieces of art. Little pieces (even miniatures) can be hung on the side of a cabinet as part of a shelf display, or even on a door for added interest throughout your home. Surprising placement of tiny artworks peppered here and there will bring you joy every time you see them.

When choosing what goes on your walls, think about the focal point of the room. Is it a large floral rug? Go a little lighter on the walls. A mural or wallpaper may not be the best choice. In our dining room, where I hand-painted large-scale florals on the wall, I chose a more "subdued" (a relative term, as I'm obviously a maximalist) rug in a geometric print for the floor.

PROJECT
fabric–covered pinboard as art

ONE VERY EASY and inexpensive way of giving your walls a little oomph is with fabric. You can stretch fabric over canvas stretcher bars, but I love stretching it over a material called soundboard. Soundboard is found in the lumber area of your local home improvement store. It's a soft and very lightweight material much like cork. Covered in fabric, it makes a beautiful display on its own, and you can use pins to tack things to it as well.

MATERIALS

A piece of fabric, cut 2 inches (5 cm)
    larger than the soundboard on all sides
A piece of soundboard, cut to your
    desired size
Handheld staple gun and staples
Optional: Four screws, one for each
    corner, if you intend to hang your board

TO MAKE:

1   Place the fabric wrong-side up on your work surface and lay the soundboard on top of it.

2   One at a time, fold each corner of the fabric over the corners of the soundboard at a 45-degree angle and staple in place.

3   One at a time, fold each edge of the fabric up and over the soundboard and staple in place about 2 to 3 inches apart.

4   Use a screw in each corner to hang the pinboard on the wall.

CHAPTER 13

using vintage florals

flea market finds and
treasured collections

Vintage florals were my gateway
to floral addiction. This probably
originated with my mom. Her
gorgeous Rose Chintz china
and Desert Rose everyday ware,
collections of floral hankies and
scarves from the 1950s, the floral tole
chandelier that hung in our house,
and the botanical carpet that went up
our front staircase . . . these blooming
visuals fill my memories.

SNAPDRAGON

The snapdragon,
named for a mythical
creature, has double
symbolism: It can
mean grace and
strength, but also
may symbolize
deviousness. White
snapdragons
symbolize purity,
grace, and
innocence, while
the purple variety
is associated with
magic and mystery.

VINTAGE FABRICS

Inspired by my mother, I collect vintage floral fabrics that I make into handbags. I love vintage feedsacks, gorgeous bark cloth (often made into draperies), old chenille blankets, and so much more.

I've made a ton of pillows from vintage fabric, and I use it on tables, as upholstery, and even as curtains. Recently I came across several yards of pristine floral fabric from the 1950s or '60s. It even had the dime-store tag still on it! I used some to trim white curtains, and you can do the same to reinvent store-bought curtains. Simply line them and then trim with vintage fabric to create a whole new look. (And since you will have saved lots of money on your curtain "upgrade," you can invest in the highest-quality rods and rings.)

SALVAGING FLORAL SCARVES

I've recently begun collecting vintage floral scarves.
These old gals are like works of art. I tie smaller ones on
vases and lamps for added detail and frame larger ones
as pieces of art. They also make incredible table toppers,
as shown below.

TRY LAYERING SEVERAL VINTAGE SCARVES to create a beautifully maximalist look. And why not place them on the backs of sofas or chairs and on beds as well?

Even just a few scarves displayed on hooks or on a blanket ladder (shown opposite) will add dimension to a room.

IF YOU HAVE a large collection of scarves, why not sew them together to make a quilt or shower curtain or window drape (as I did for this daybed nook)?

A SINGLE BEAUTIFUL scarf can make a gorgeous pillow—or sew several scarves together to create a unique table runner or tablecloth. I even framed one as wall art.

REPURPOSING VINTAGE TABLEWARE

A collection of mismatched vintage floral plates sets a stunning table, but they invite display on more than just the tabletop. Stacks of vintage goodness on open shelves are alluring and atmospheric, too.

PLATES MAKE FOR GORGEOUS wall displays. Try using them in unexpected spots: I use a vintage serving dish for jewelry on my vanity (see following spread). And instead of having the box of detergent on top of my washer, I pour the detergent into a glass jar and use a floral teacup as a scoop. I took the dryer sheets out of the box as well and set them on a vintage floral plate. Why have something ugly sitting around when you can have something pretty?

SAVING BLOOMING VINTAGE
NEEDLEPOINT AND EMBROIDERY

Oh my goodness, do I ever love a nice grannie needle-point. They make incredible pillows and upholstery.

VINTAGE EPHEMERA

Vintage botanical prints, scraps of old wallpaper, and ephemera can be used in displays all over the house. You can frame these items or just create a pretty collage somewhere. Anything made of paper can be decoupaged onto a trunk, a table, a dresser . . . pretty much anything you can think of! Even the little scraps of needlepoints and embroidery can be combined with newer fabrics, as on this pillow I made for my niece.

VINTAGE FLORAL TINS

Vintage floral tins are one of my favorite items to collect. They're usually relatively inexpensive and easy to find at local vintage and thrift shops. I put small plants in these, use them to hold flower bouquets (with a glass vase or plastic cup inside so they don't rust or leak), and also use them simply for storage and display.

pattern notebook:
vintage gift wrap or wallpaper tablecloths, runners, and place mats

I love repurposing vintage items for tablescapes. Beautiful vintage wallpaper is among my favorite things to play with. You can place a long piece across a table as a runner. Or cut the paper into place mats as I did in my dining room. Mix papers, including wallpapers and gift wrap and even scrapbook papers, both old and new, for a unique look. Imagine the gold metallic vintage wallpaper pictured here spread across the table for New Year's Eve, or the florals for spring holidays or showers! Place mats are, in general, sized either 12 x 18 or 14 x 20 inches (30 x 45 cm or 35 x 50 cm). I use a long plastic ruler meant for quilting and a rotary cutter on a cutting mat to cut out place mats, instead of fiddling with scissors. You could also use a straight edge and a box cutter. If you like to entertain like I do, grab gorgeous vintage gift wrap and wallpaper when you see it!

using vintage florals

bari j. ackerman

I'M AN ARTIST, but I didn't always create art. As a very visual person, I was a fashionista sort in high school, and I was crazy for interior design. But I was busy singing and dancing and being an actress. I never ever thought I could make art. My mom was the artist. I was the actress. That was that.

And though I started college as a theater major, I graduated with a degree in social sciences and women's studies. Not really related to art, I'd say. Out of college, I worked in advertising.

I came to art in my early thirties as a way to express myself. When my now almost-grown girls were young, I was always puttering around. I wanted our home to be different—I didn't want it to look like a page from a home décor catalog. I wanted it to look like us. And I also didn't want to dress from a catalog. I started making jewelry from found objects and then collages. Soon I was sewing handbags for my own small business, Bari J.

Eventually, I decided I needed my own fabric for the handbags, so I taught myself to design fabric using illustration software. A year later, I licensed my first line of fabric. It was a painterly line called "Full Bloom" that most people assumed I had painted by hand (I hadn't). For years I continued to create art with the computer . . . and then I made the leap to paint. I was hooked.

Now, years later, I know what was always true: I am an artist. And I am a painter.

Since that first fabric line, I have created seventeen collections of fabric and art for wallpaper, home décor, wall art, rugs, and much more.

resources

A full, page by page resource list is on Bari's website at barijdesigns.com/pages/bloom-wild-resources.

Bari J. fabric is manufactured by Art Gallery Fabrics and is available at fabric shops worldwide. See barijdesigns.com/pages/where-to-find-my-fabric.

You can find sources for Bari J. wallpaper, bedding, stencils, and murals, as well as Bari J. paintings and prints, at barijdesigns.com.

Bari J. rugs are made by Loloi Rugs and are part of the Wild Bloom collection. They can be found at such retailers as Anthropologie and Grandin Road, anthropologie.com, grandinroad.com.

Most of the vintage items in this book were sourced from Etsy, as well as many thrift and antique shops.

The pink sofa pictured throughout the book was provided by Joybird, joybird.com.

The rattan headboard, carved wood side table, lanterns, and many of the velvet pillows in this book were provided by Tierra Del Lagarto, Scottsdale, Arizona.

The upholstery is by Sit Well Upholstery, Phoenix, Arizona.

The yellow midcentury chaise is from Modern Manor, Phoenix, Arizona.

Fabric covered lampshade was purchased from Ballard Designs, ballarddesigns.com and recovered by Kim Martucci of Brimfield Awakening, brimfieldawakening.com.

Sage bundles custom created by Lindsey Oldani of Notable Normalcy.

Flowers are from Mayesh Wholesale.

Some of the vintage dinnerware is from my own collection and some is from Fancy Lou, fancylou.com.

Custom dining room curtains by J & M Creations.

Vintage floral paintings mostly sourced from Elsie Green, elsiegreen.com.

acknowledgments

MOST OF THE STYLING IN THIS BOOK was done by or overseen by my dear friend and stylist Sarah Ehlinger. Frankly, she is a superwoman. In addition to styling, she supervised the entire photo shoot, ensuring we got everything done on time and beautifully. Sarah also was the person who encouraged me most along the way. This book would not be the same without her. Sarah, I am infinitely grateful for you in every way!

Special thank-you to my sweet husband, Kevin, who long ago was dubbed Super Husband because he can build or fix anything. When it came to this book, he hung a ton of wallpaper with only a little complaining, built things, and, most of all, tolerated me when I was extremely intolerable. Love you, Kevin!

I'd also like to thank photographer Carley Summers, whose keen eye and collaborative spirit made my vision of this book come to life.

Additionally, a huge thank-you to my agent, Alison Fargis, for believing in me and encouraging me. I know for a fact this book would not be published without her. And a huge thank-you to the editor of *Bloom Wild*, Shawna Mullen. Shawna's endless kindness, creativity, encouragement, professionalism, and immense knowledge made this book more than I ever dreamed it could be.